CLASSIC CARS
AN IMAGINATION LIBRARY SERIES

THE STORY OF

Chevy
Corvettes

by David K. Wright

Gareth Stevens Publishing
A WORLD ALMANAC EDUCATION GROUP COMPANY

Please visit our web site at: www.garethstevens.com
For a free color catalog describing Gareth Stevens Publishing's
list of high-quality books and multimedia programs,
call 1-800-542-2595 (USA) or 1-800-387-3178 (Canada).
Gareth Stevens Publishing's fax: (414) 332-3567.

Library of Congress Cataloging-in-Publication Data

Wright, David K.
 The story of Chevy Corvettes / by David K. Wright.
  p. cm. — (Classic cars: an imagination library series)
 Includes bibliographical references and index.
 Summary: Traces the development of one of America's most popular
sports cars, the Corvette, and describes the changes in various models
over the years.
  ISBN 0-8368-3189-6 (lib. bdg.)
  1. Corvette automobile—Juvenile literature. [1. Corvette automobile—
History.] I. Title.
TL215.C6W75 2002
629.222'2—dc21   2002067045

First published in 2002 by
Gareth Stevens Publishing
A World Almanac Education Group Company
330 West Olive Street, Suite 100
Milwaukee, WI 53212 USA

Text: David K. Wright
Cover design and page layout: Scott M. Krall
Series editor: Jim Mezzanotte
Picture Researcher: Diane Laska-Swanke

Photo credits: Cover, pp. 5, 13, 17 © Ron Kimball; pp. 7, 9, 11, 15, 19, 21 Courtesy of
Mid America Designs, Inc.

Printed in the United States of America

2 3 4 5 6 7 8 9 06 05 04

*Front cover: By the 1960s, Chevy Corvettes
were well known for their power and speed.
This Corvette is a 1963 Stingray coupe.*

TABLE OF CONTENTS

Words that appear in the glossary are printed in **boldface** type the first time they occur in the text.

THE FIRST CORVETTES

In the early fifties, Chevrolet made many popular cars. "Chevy" cars were cheap and reliable, but most of them were also slow and not very exciting. An **engineer** named Harley Earl had an idea for a more exciting Chevy. It was a small, two-seat sports car called the Corvette. The Corvette looked fast just standing still.

Chevrolet began selling the Corvette in 1953. It had an unusual body that was made of **fiberglass** instead of metal. The first Corvette looked great, but it was too slow. Chevrolet put a more powerful engine in the car and made it more fun to drive. By 1959, Corvettes were winning races!

When this 1953 Corvette left the factory, it looked different than it does now! The car's owner has added special wheels and a special paint job.

STINGRAY!

In 1963, Chevrolet introduced a new Corvette called the Stingray. It was named after a wide, smooth fish with a stinging tail. The car still had a fiberglass body, but it looked much different than the previous model. It was low and sleek, and it had headlights hidden behind special panels.

The new Corvette did not just look different. It was also much faster! Chevrolet put huge, powerful engines in Stingrays. These engines used a lot of gasoline, but most people did not mind because gas was so cheap. Many people bought Stingray **convertibles**. It was fun to drive a Stingray with the top down!

This Corvette Stingray is from 1963, the first year the model was sold. It has a long hood to hold its huge engine and big exhaust pipes under the doors.

FASTER AND FASTER

On the racetrack, racing Corvettes sounded like thunder. They seemed to make the ground shake! These cars were **modified** for racing. They had special engines and wheels, and they also had metal bars over the driver's head for protection in accidents. Big scoops in the hoods brought air to the engines.

Fans everywhere watched the Corvettes race and win. The cars won on courses that curved through the countryside, and they won on huge ovals. They also won at drag strips. This success helped Chevrolet sell more cars. The company's **motto** was "win on Sunday, sell on Monday."

Racing Corvettes look much different than regular models. This 1968 Corvette has special wheels and tires, wide fenders, and bars to protect the driver.

THE LAST CONVERTIBLE

In 1973, gasoline became more expensive in the United States. People began buying small cars from Japan and Europe, because the cars used very little gasoline. Cars that used a lot of gas, such as the Corvette, became less popular.

At the same time, safety became more important. To make Corvettes safer, Chevrolet put steel beams in the doors and extra padding in the **interiors**.

After 1975, Chevrolet stopped making convertible Corvettes and sold only hardtops. The hardtops were safer than the convertibles, so **insurance** for the cars cost less money. Many people missed the noisy but fun convertible.

This 1975 Corvette has a hard top that protects people if the car rolls over. It also has hidden headlights that pop up from inside the hood.

TWENTY-FIVE YEARS OF CORVETTES

By 1978, Corvettes had been around for twenty-five years. Even though Corvettes did not have small, **efficient** engines, a lot of people loved owning and driving these fast, exciting sports cars. When Chevrolet introduced a special, twenty-fifth anniversary model in 1978, thousands wanted to buy it!

Chevrolet also introduced another special model in 1978. The model was based on the Corvette **pace car** that led racing cars around the track at the start of the famous Indianapolis 500 auto race. This Corvette was black and silver, with special badges, stripes, and decals.

In 1978, Chevrolet introduced this special "Indy Pace Car" Corvette. People who drove this car could imagine they were at the Indianapolis 500!

TIME FOR A CHANGE

Even though many people loved the Corvette, by the early 1980s the car was ready for a change. So in 1984, Chevrolet introduced a new Corvette. It was called the C4.

The C4 was a completely new design. It had many parts made of lightweight **aluminum**, so it weighed less than previous Corvettes and used less gas. The C4 could also go around corners very fast.

Although the C4 was more expensive than previous Corvettes, it was a big hit — especially when Chevrolet introduced a convertible model in 1986! A new, state-of-the art factory in Kentucky built the new Corvette.

These C4 Corvettes are getting ready to race! The C4 model was much different than previous Corvettes. It was lighter and handled better.

A BRAND NEW CAR

Year after year, Chevrolet kept improving the Corvette. The company offered more powerful engines, and it made more comfortable seats, smoother bodies, and prettier wheels. In the 1990s, however, engineers at Chevrolet began designing a new, better Corvette.

In 1997, Chevrolet began selling a new model called the C5. Everything about the C5 was a new design, from its **sophisticated** engine to its smooth, plastic body. The car had even better handling and greater speed than the C4, but it was also easy to drive around town. Many people think the C5 is the best Corvette yet!

The C5 is a new design, but it has some things in common with older Corvettes. It has hidden headlights, for example, and a powerful engine.

EVERYBODY LOVES CORVETTES

Corvettes have many **devoted** fans! Corvette owners look for any excuse to drive their cars. Many Corvette owners belong to local Corvette clubs, and they enter their cars in parades and car shows. They love to drive, talk about, and show off their Corvettes.

Some people prefer older Corvettes because the cars remind them of when they were young. Many like to **restore** these older cars so they are just like new. Today, older Corvettes are worth a lot of money.

A Corvette car show usually has models from all different years. Here, an early Corvette is parked next to some later models.

THE CORVETTE OF TOMORROW

Today's Corvette is a wonderful car, but what will tomorrow's Corvette be like? At this very moment, engineers at Chevrolet are designing a Corvette for the future. Will it have a plastic body? What kind of engine will it have? How fast will it be?

At automobile **exhibitions**, Corvette show cars give people a glimpse of the future. With these one-of-a-kind cars, engineers from Chevrolet show off their latest ideas. No matter how it looks or runs, the Corvette of tomorrow will certainly be exciting!

This Corvette show car has a very special door! It opens upward, like the wing of a bird. Will the Corvette of tomorrow have this kind of door?

MORE TO READ AND VIEW

Books (Nonfiction)   *Corvette. Ultimate Cars* (series). A. T. McKenna
(Abdo & Daughters Publishing)
Corvette: America's Sports Car. Randy Leffingwell
(Motorbooks International)
Corvettes. Great American Muscle Cars (series).
Eric Ethan (Gareth Stevens)
Corvettes. High Performance (series). Kal Gronvall
(Capstone Press)
Corvettes: The Cars That Created the Legend.
Dennis Adler (Krause Publications)

Videos (Nonfiction)   *Corvette.* (Best Film & Video)
Driving Passion: America's Love Affair with the Car,
Part 3 — Golden Age of Detroit. (Turner Home Entertainment)
The Visual History of Cars: Corvette. (MPI Home Video)

PLACES TO WRITE AND VISIT

Here are three places to contact for more information:

Corvette Americana
Hall of Fame
Rt. 28
Cooperstown, NY 13326
USA
1-607-547-4135

Mid America Designs, Inc.
P.O. Box 1368
Effingham, IL 62401
USA
1-800-500-VETT (8388)
www.madirect.com

National Corvette Museum
350 Corvette Dr.
Bowling Green, KY 42101
USA
1-800-538-3883
www.corvettemuseum.com

WEB SITES

Web sites change frequently, but we believe the following web sites are going to last. You can also use good search engines, such as **Yahooligans!** [www.yahooligans.com] or **Google** [www.google.com], to find more information about Chevy Corvettes. Here are some keywords to help you: *Chevrolet, Chevy, Corvette, Harley Earl, Stingray, Zora Arkus-Duntov,* and *ZR-1.*

www.chevrolet.com/corvette/index.htm

This is the official Chevrolet web site. Visit this site to learn about all the latest Corvette models and see some nice photos.

www.corvette.net

The person who hosts this web site must really like the 1966 Corvette! This site has a lot of pictures of Corvettes, and it also has pictures of the cars being put together.

www.corvetteclubofamerica.com

The *Corvette Club of America* hosts this web site. It has a lot of information about upcoming Corvette shows.

www.corvettecrew.com

Many different Corvettes are bought and sold on this web site. Find out which models are hard to find.

www.corvettemuseum.com/pictures/special_display/index.shtml

Special Displays is part of the web site hosted by the *National Corvette Museum.* It has pictures of many different Corvettes from the 1950s, 1960s, and 1970s.

www.vettenet.org/grlist.html

Pictures of Corvettes is part of the *Vette Net* web site. Visit it to see many interesting photos of Corvettes from all different years.

www.zlx.com/Corvette

This web site is called *Corvette Legends.* Visit this site to learn about the 2002 Corvette Z06, the fastest Corvette ever! The site also has information about other Corvette models, from the earliest to the latest.

GLOSSARY

You can find these words on the pages listed. Reading a word in a sentence helps you understand it even better.

aluminum (uh-LUME-in-uhm) — a type of metal that is strong but lightweight 14

convertibles (con-VERT-uh-bulls) — cars with tops that can be folded back or removed 6, 10, 14

devoted (duh-VOTE-ed) — very loyal 18

efficient (ef-ISH-unt) — able to do a job without wasting a lot of time, energy, or materials 12

engineer (ehn-jin-EAR) — a person who plans the construction of structures or machines, such as cars 4, 16, 20

exhibitions (ecks-ih-BISH-uns) — public shows or demonstrations 20

fiberglass (FYE-ber-glas) — a material made of thin glass threads and plastic that can be molded into different shapes 4, 6

insurance (in-SURE-unts) — a contract that guarantees, for a certain amount of money, that something will be fixed or replaced in case of an accident 10

interiors (in-TEAR-e-urz) — the inside spaces of things, such as houses or cars 10

modified (MOD-if-eyed) — changed from the original 8

motto (MOT-oh) — a saying 8

pace car (PAYCE car) — a car that leads racing cars around a track just before a race starts to establish a certain speed 12

restore (ree-STOR) — to fix something so it is back to its original condition 18

sophisticated (so-FIS-ta-cay-tud) — being complicated or using the newest ideas 16

INDEX